FINDING
God
IN AUTISM

A forty day devotional for the Parents of Autistic Children.

KATHY MEDINA

Tate Publishing & Enterprises

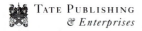

TATE PUBLISHING
& Enterprises

"Finding God in Autism–A 40 Day Devotional for Parents of Autistic Spectrum Children"
by Kathy Medina
Copyright © 2006 by Kathy Medina. All rights reserved.

Published in the United States of America
by Tate Publishing, LLC
127 East Trade Center Terrace
Mustang, OK 73064
(888) 361-9473

Scripture quotations marked "NIV" are taken from the Holy Bible, New International Version ®, Copyright © 1973, 1978, 1984 by International Bible Society. Used by permission of Zondervan Publishing House. All rights reserved.

The opinions expressed by the author are not necessarily those of Tate Publishing, LLC.

This book is designed to provide accurate and authoritative information with regard to the subject matter covered. This information is given with the understanding that neither the author nor Tate Publishing, LLC is engaged in rendering legal, professional advice. Since the details of your situation are fact dependent, you should additionally seek the services of a competent professional.

Cover design by Janae Glass
Interior design by Melissa Griggs

ISBN: 1-5988656-3-3
06.07.13

I DEDICATE THIS BOOK TO
Jake, Zack and Lexi

"'For I know the plans I have for you,' declares the Lord, 'Plans to prosper you and not to harm you, plans to give you hope and a future. Then you will call upon Me and come and pray to Me and I will listen to you. You will seek Me and find Me when you seek me with all your heart. I will be found by you.' Declares the Lord, 'and will bring you back from captivity." Jeremiah 29:11-14

May you always turn to Jesus…He'll never leave you or let you down.

With all my love,Mom

Acknowledgments

To Zack... You have done more for my personal and spiritual growth than anyone! You have pushed me to my knees and forced me to learn the computer to find answers for you! I love you and will never stop praying and circling the globe for answers to help you in your recovery from autism. Someday, we will sit in heaven and have a feast and you will be allowed to eat everything that is served...oh, how I look forward to that day. I long to see you eat all you want without any consequences!!!

To Glenn... My husband and the love of my life. Together we've grown in all areas of our life. We knew our lives would change when we had children, but we didn't know to what extent! I'd marry you all over again!

To Jake and Lexi... You're refreshing, easy and two terrific kids! I love you...dad and I would do no less for you than what we do for your brother.

To Mom and Dad... You gave me the foundation and the example to follow Jesus. I wouldn't be doing well if you hadn't taught me what you did. Your rewards will be many in heaven for what you have done for Zack and me. God gave me the best when He gave me you!

To Sheri and Todd... Thanks for the roses! Your tutoring, love and prayers have sustained me.

To Mark, Steve and Rebekah... Thanks for tutoring, babysitting and giving Zack your unconditional love. He is a well deserving nephew!

To Dr. Jerry Kartzinel... We prayed you into our life to help us help our son. You are the brains in helping us understand and heal Zack's gut. Your love for the Lord and autistic children is a testimony all of its own.

To the MELT Sunday School Class... You put up with Zack's noises in class and you accept him for where he is. You have helped us financially, you have fixed things in our home that Zack has broken and you still remain our friends! Your prayers are working and we love each and every one of you!

To Sharon and Kent Hames... We prayed for four years before God brought you into our lives! You stepped up to help us when no one else would. You will be greatly rewarded in heaven for loving Zack and not judging him. You are a blessing beyond words.

To Linda... You are the most supportive, inspirational mother I know! You taught me how to culture foods and to explore treatments that were new to me. I miss you living so close to me. Here is to our boys recovering from autism! I love you!

To My Tutors... Whether you are with me now or you have tutored in the past...each and every one of you have made a significant difference forever in Zack's life. You have taught him many skills that may not have come to him if you hadn't been in our home. You each have a part in Zack's recovery. I know you are forever changed knowing Zack like he is forever changed in knowing you.

To Amy Prince MA, CCC-SLP... You are the only speech therapist to make notable gains with our son. You are a jewel in your field. You are the best and I would recommend you to anyone!

To Meg Shapiro... Thank you for helping Zack with Cranio-Sacral treatments. Your dedication to special needs children is unmatched by anyone. You are helping so many kids lead a better life. God bless.

To Allison Zevallos... Keep teaching us the RDI way! Its working and another piece to this huge puzzle we are putting together!

I GAVE GOD FORTY DAYS AND ALL OF ME

It had been a rough couple of months and I could see no light at the end of my tunnel. Our son didn't seem to be making any noticeable improvements on the new supplements we had him on. He had no new academic gains and Sundays were the worst day of my week. My husband took our two other children to church on a Sunday morning while I sat at home with our son Zack. He could not sit through church without disturbing others. I turned on the television and tuned into TBN. A loud, obnoxious preacher came on screaming the gospel at me. I prayed to God to help me stop judging him and listen to what God might have to say to me that morning.

The preacher said God was the same yesterday, today and tomorrow. If I wasn't feeling close to God then it was me who moved away, not God. The sermon was about raising my personal commitment to God. It encouraged believers to take forty days and do something to strengthen our relationship with God. He promised God would move when I decided to move! What did I have to lose? I knew if I did nothing, that in forty days, I would be in the same place I was currently in. I did not like the prospect of that idea!

I decided to do three things that would be difficult for me to do on a day in and a day out basis, and committed to do these three things for forty consecutive days. This is what I promised to do. First, I promised to read my Bible every single day. Seven days a week and reading in church on Sunday did not count! I committed to having a personal study with God every single day for forty days. Second, I committed to laying hands on our son and praying in my prayer language every night for forty consecutive nights. After our son was asleep, I would kneel by his bedside and pray while laying my hands on him. Third, I committed to taking communion and remembering what Christ's bloodshed did for me every single night for forty consecutive days. I picked this because since I missed so many Sunday's, I could not remember the last time I took communion and it was something I truly missed!

I wrote my three commitments down on paper and put them in an envelope. I didn't tell anyone what I set out to do. I went to the grocery store and bought a box of crackers and a bottle of grape juice. The next night I began to work on my promise to God. I set no time limit. Some nights I was done in thirty minutes and other nights I spent more than an hour in prayer, Bible reading and communion. My outlook on life changed. My attitude changed, my hope rose high and the truth I knew about God and His promises was strengthened beyond what I had hoped for.

In one of my early prayer times, I told God I really wanted two rose trees for our backyard. They are low maintenance and beautiful to look at and would add a lot of color to our yard. At fifty dollars a rose tree, there was no money in the budget for two rose trees for our yard. Our son's medical treatments and hiring tutors to teach him were costing us so much each month. I could not justify spending one hundred dollars on two rose trees. I prayed and asked God if He could find a way, I would be grateful.

One day I read Psalm 23: "The Lord is my shepherd, I shall lack nothing. He makes me lie down in green pastures, He leads me beside quiet waters, He restores my soul. He guides me in paths of righteousness for His name's sake. Even though I walk through the valley of the shadow of death, I will fear no evil, for you are with me: your rod and your staff, they comfort me. You prepare a table before me in the presence of my enemies. You anoint my head with oil: my cup overflows.

8

Surely goodness and love will follow me all the days of my life, and I will dwell in the house of the Lord forever."

What stood out to me was verse five "…my cup overflows…" I have many blessings in life, but never could I think of a time when my cup overflowed with a blessing! Never did I say, "Stop Lord, that's enough of a blessing! I can't handle anymore, please stop blessing me!" That night I prayed, "Lord, sometime in my life time I would like to experience a blessing from You where my cup overflowed!" I want to say, "Stop, that's enough of a blessing Lord!" I was intrigued God could bless any of us so much we would ask Him to stop the blessing!

Being in God's word on a daily basis heightened my hope for Zack's recovery. I meditated on God's promises. I memorized His promises. I chose to take God at His word, and wonderful things began to happen. Tutoring our son was less of a chore. I slept better at night. I worried less about finances and Zack's future. I was stronger, more confident every day. On days when I didn't feel like fulfilling my commitment I talked myself into doing it! "Just ten more straight days, Kathy! Then, I will know if the TV preacher was right!" Would God, reveal Himself to me in a new way?

For two years we had been doing an ABA home school program with Zack. Within the ABA program is a program called Receptive Object Labels. We put a shoe and a ball on the table and said, "Zack, touch shoe." or "Zack, touch ball." For two years we asked him this about fifty times a day. He never got above fifty percent. He was always guessing. He did not know what a shoe or what a ball was. It was boring to keep asking him. It was frustrating. How could I ever tell him to go get his shoes and socks if he didn't even know what a shoe or a sock was? He had no concept that things had a label.

On day thirty-eight of my commitment, I went into the tutor room to work with our son. I started with the receptive object label program. I asked Zack to touch the shoe, he touched the shoe! I asked him to touch the ball, he touched the ball! I asked him to hand me the shoe, he handed me the shoe! I did the same with the ball, he handed me the ball! I mixed the two objects up, he answered right every time! I used different balls and different shoes. Every time I asked, he got it right! He not only learned the names of ball and a shoe but he learned to generalize the items as well. When another tutor came over I was so excited when he got every answer right with her too! I called my mother over, she asked Zack, and Zack was one hundred percent right every time she asked!

That was a major break through for our son. He learned five new objects every day after that until he learned the name of 2,000 objects in less than a year later! He had no problem ever generalizing about an object. If we showed him a picture of a tree, he instinctively knew that trees came in a lot of different shapes, sizes and colors.

I was excited to go to Bible study that night and share with others what God had done! I raised my commitment to God and He brought a new skill to our son. I couldn't be happier and wanted to share the testimony. As I was close to leaving for Bible study the telephone rang. It was my sister.

My sister lives about forty-five minutes away. She and her husband own a feed lot with about 4,000 cows. She asked me, "Kathy, do you want any rose trees?"

"Sure! Why do you have one?" I asked.

"Yes, as a matter of fact I do! How many do you want?"

"I'll take two!!" I said.

"Is that all you want?" she asked.

I was stunned, only my husband knew I wanted two rose trees for our backyard. "Three? I don't know, what is going on, Sheri?"

"Look, I'll be in town tonight and I will bring some rose trees by and I will explain it all to you later." she told me. I told her I would be at Bible study but Glenn would be home and I would call her later.

I went to Bible study and shared with the girls what God had done for Zack and when I got home, I thought there would be rose trees waiting for me! When I came home, there were thirty-five rose trees in my two bath tubs!!!! I was more than shocked; I didn't understand what was happening. I called my sister up immediately and asked her where she got so many rose trees!

My sister giggled as she told me about her day! She said her husband Todd loved roses and one of his good friends had been in town shopping at a local nursery. When the owner of the nursery saw his big truck (many cowboys have big trucks!) the owner approached him. The owner thought he bought way too many rose trees this season and he needed to dump them. He had sold them at regular price, ran a huge sale and still he had 4,000 rose trees left. He couldn't lower his price anymore or he would offend his regular customers. He offered Todd's friend $500 to take them to the local dump for him.

Being a young twenty year old, Todd's friend jumped on the opportunity! Once the rose trees were loaded up on his truck, he decided to take the rose trees to Todd's 200 acre feedlot. He knew Todd loved roses and thought the feedlot would look better lined with thousands of rose trees! He sold all the rose trees to Todd for $500. Smart young man!

Later that day, Todd thought about the man power it would take to plant 4,000 rose bushes! Even with tractors, the job would take too long and the rose trees would die if not planted soon. So, Sheri and Todd called up each relative and offered each of us rose trees! A gift to us.

I started to cry. I knew they were a gift from God routed through my brother-in-law. I asked Sheri to put Todd on the telephone. I shared with them my commitment to God the last thirty-eight days. They knew they were part of a plan that God set about to bless all of us.

The next day, I set out with a shovel and started planting rose trees in my back and front yard. It took most of the day. My husband wanted to help but I said, "No thanks. This one is for me to do!" I planted all but two rose trees. My yard was full! I went inside my house to call my friend, Pat. I wanted to give her the two last rose trees. There was no answer at her house. I hung up and started to cry. I prayed and said, "No more God. It's too much. My cup is running over! Stop the blessing, I have more than enough!" I realized God had been listening to my heartfelt prayers. He wanted to bless me like I wanted to be blessed. I drew closer to Him and I knew it. I dug up a big green bush in the backyard and threw it away. I planted the last two rose trees.

I have physical reminders every day whether I am in my front yard or my back yard of how God blesses me every day of the year. They die, they bloom again. The rose trees bloom profusely. People always comment on my beautiful roses and I tell everyone how God gave them to me.

After it all sunk in, my family and I talked about this blessing. God had been waiting for me to be faithful to Him. He set this blessing in motion long before I started my 40 day commitment to Him. The owner of the nursery never could have over ordered rose trees to begin with. What made him order so many rose trees to begin with? Had I not kept my commitment, Todd's friend may not have ever been offered the chance to haul the rose trees to the dump. Todd could have planted all 4,000 trees and not offered any to me or other family members. Each group of families in our circle of relatives had one person currently tutoring our son. God blessed everyone who had a hand in helping Zack improve. How many blessings have I missed out on because I have been too selfish, too lazy or too busy to turn to God? More than I care to think about!!!!

Why Forty?

What is so special about giving God forty consecutive days? I really wanted to know, so the research began. The number forty occurs quite often in the Bible. God has stamped numbers on all of His creation. He has woven them into His Word. In the Bible, numbers are used with great precision. They help us see the supernatural design in the mind of God.

Israel wandered in the wilderness for forty years (Duet. 8:2-5; Psalm 95:10). Moses spent forty years, in Egypt, learning to be somebody in Pharaohs courts. Then he spent the next forty years learning to be nobody in the desert. His last forty years he spent learning that God was all He said He was, and He guided Israel out of Egypt and into the Promise Land of Canaan.

Saul was given forty years to prove himself fit to be worthy to be the king of Israel. He was rejected by God for all his rebellion.

Jonah was to preach to Nineveh; the city had forty days to prepare itself for the coming of God's wrath. Jesus was tempted by Satan for forty consecutive days. Jesus stayed on earth for forty days after His resurrection to prove to everyone He rose again.

Jesus fasted from food for forty days. Elijah fasted from food for forty days as well. Moses fasted from food for forty days on two different occasions. The flood that covered the earth while Noah was in the Ark was for forty days.

Moses stayed on the Mount Sinai for forty days; he was fasting from food when he received God's laws, the Ten Commandments. In the book of Judges, the Israelite confederation suffered 40 years of harassment at the hands of the Philistines (Judges 13:1). David and Solomon both ruled Israel for forty years each.

Forty days can be considered a season. When you commit to praying for your child and studying God's word for forty consecutive days you have entered into a season that will bring forth a harvest. Satan came to kill, steal and destroy us. We need God's Almighty power to overcome.

I hope you will give God the next forty days of your life and allow Him to strengthen you as you pray for yourself and your child. As you learn more about God and His unfailing promises, you will feel more peace and hope.

The God we serve is a God who keeps His promises. The Bible is filled with promises for us to know and experience. Numbers 23:19 says, "God is not a man, that he should lie, nor a son of man, that he should change his mind. Does He speak and then not act? Does He promise and not fulfill? God is incapable of reneging on His written Word."

We parents of children with special needs can get very desperate to help our children. Desperation makes us vulnerable. Vulnerable to many false healings. Autism reminded me how much I needed God. I need Him more than ever…don't you? If you have accepted Christ as your Lord and Savior then let me remind you we serve a jealous God. God warns us against worshipping idols. (If you haven't already accepted Christ into your heart, in the back of this book is a prayer that can help you make Christ real in your life; the sinner's prayer.)

When God is jealous, it is not of what we may worship. He is jealous for us. He wants us to stay focused on Him and put our faith, trust and hope in Him. God knows that 'other gods' of this world are nothing. Other gods cannot deliver what they promise. No other has conquered the grave. No other is worthy of our praise.

On this journey I have seen many desperate parents wanting to do something to help their child. When you have been looking for your miracle, and you can't hear God's voice, it is very hard to wait out God's silence. When God doesn't seem to answer, it is easy to look elsewhere for answers. When you go somewhere other than God, you open yourself up to the devil's schemes and lies. I have seen parents fall victim to thinking that anything is better than riding out God's silence. Parents justify crazy treatments as harmless and believe if it can't hurt their child, then it is worth a try. But in many cultures doing these rituals means you are worshiping their god.

Here are a few rituals I have come across. Rubbing Buddha's tummy, having children drink blessed salt water, parents sending telepathic words to their children to gain language, chanting cultural prayers, waving incense over their sleeping child, taking their children to temples, and participating in séances. I have run across parents seeking answers in different religions and parents combining many different religions desperate for someone somewhere to reach out and heal their child. All in false efforts to help their children overcome autism. It disappoints God when we don't have enough faith in Him, and Him alone, to heal our children. We must remember that it was God who shut the lions mouths, parted the Red Sea and raised Christ up from the dead...He can heal our children of autism.

I started to stray a few times in my commitment and believed no harm could come to our son. I was persuaded by well meaning, loving parents. Nobody wants to pursue a wacky treatment alone, so they often solicit another parent to join them! Family members pulled me back and reminded me to wait on God. It is in the times of no change, good or bad that Satan tempts us. We cannot react to God's silence or delays by trying to help Him out and speed up the healing process. Maybe God is being silent so we will use up our resources! After we exhaust all other avenues, maybe we will finally realize we are hopeless without Him.

I have heard on more than one occasion people tell me that their god is the universe. They are open to whomever and whatever brings something good. Let me tell you, that is a very dangerous way of thinking. Make no mistake, if you open yourself up to whatever is out there...garbage is going to come in. Stick with following Christ; it is the right road to be on to help our children recover from autism.

If you are looking for a landmark improvement for your child, then I invite you to draw closer to God. What will God do for you? I do not know. But when you commit time to God, you will be changed. You will become stronger. You will be at peace. God will bless you and give you the deepest desires of your heart. God longs to give us the desires of our hearts.

Before our son was diagnosed with autism, my night stand and coffee table was filled with Home and Garden books and magazines. Then autism came into our lives and those books and magazines were replaced with autism research material. I became so overwhelmed and weary. I replaced three-fourths of those books with Bible study material and my Bible.

I know what it feels like to be tired, overwhelmed and scared. You must believe if you make a sacrifice that is necessary to seek out God, you will be rewarded. Life will get easier and your child will get better.

Following are some suggestions to help you draw close to God and see His blessings on your life in forty days. Think of three things for God that you do not already do on a daily basis. Commit to doing these three things for the next forty consecutive days. Day in, day out, Sundays included…no excuses accepted. Here are some ideas for you to choose from: open up your Bible and read it, lay hands on your child every night when they are asleep and pray over them, take communion, hold hands and pray with your spouse, worship God in song, in your quiet prayer time raise your hands up to God, pray to receive a prayer language and pray in a prayer language, get on your knees when you pray, and keep a prayer journal. Whatever three things you decide to commit to; do them for forty consecutive days.

Decide when a good time is for you to fulfill your commitment. You might choose mornings, evenings or in the waiting room of your child's therapy sessions. We are not to expect God to give to us if we won't give Him some of our time. God is waiting to bless you and your child. He is the same yesterday, today and tomorrow. He is waiting for us to commit to Him. Direct your prayers to God and no one else. Turn a deaf ear to anything that is not in line with the Bible's teachings. Pray, do your part and wait to hear from God. God doesn't disappoint His children.

You may have a child that has a new diagnosis of autism or a child that was diagnosed many, many years ago. You may have a child that does not have autism but some other special need. No matter their age or diagnosis…the Bible's promises are for each of them and you. You are their parent and God has some encouraging words for you. Come, do this study with me!

FINDING *God* IN AUTISM

Day #1

"Do not conform any longer to the pattern of this world, but be transformed by the renewing of your mind. Then you will be able to test and approve what God's will is – His good, pleasing and perfect will."

Romans 12:2

The word conform means to pattern after, fashion after or mold after. The word transformed means changed in form.

For over a year after our son was diagnosed with autism and Neurofibromatosis Type 1, I was so frozen with disbelief and disappointment; the fear in my mind became my greatest enemy. My thoughts became more negative with each passing week. I never fell into a depression but I sure bought into the hopeless words of our son's doctors and teachers. I just couldn't bring myself to think the professionals might be wrong. I had allowed my mind to be transformed to what the professionals were telling me about our son.

The Bible teaches us to renew our minds. I had to learn to think like Christ and stop having my mind enslave our son's future. I am thankful I always believed God doesn't waste a human life. To have a son who would never talk, never behave, never think, always be a burden to someone seemed cruel and out of God's plan. Surely, our son could be of some value sometime in his lifetime! I never lost sight of that. I chose to believe God at His word.

God wasn't answering my prayers like I thought He should. I wanted Him to wipe the autism and Neurofibromatosis out of our son's life. I wanted to wake up and have my son know how to talk! My prayers were heartfelt and my faith was larger than a grain of mustard seed…so where was God's power?

In time, I learned that most of the time, God's answers come when we take action. God wanted me to read Scriptures more, read books about autism, talk with doctors, therapists and do my research. I made a conscience choice to renew my mind with Scriptures and hope returned. I asked God to transform my way of thinking. I asked God to let me see our son like He saw our son. I prayed to God to mold my way of thinking and to bring me hope.

As I prayed, the bondage in my mind started to lose its grip. I started seeing our son's potential by looking at him like Christ sees him. He was not a lost, helpless soul. He is a child of God. Pray today and ask God to renew your mind. Return your hope. To see His will. Someday we will know how perfect His plan really is for our children and ourselves.

Day #2

"Jesus asked the boy's father, 'How long has he been like this?'
'From childhood,' he answered. It has often thrown him into fire
or water to kill him. But if you can do anything, take pity on us
and help us. If you can?' said Jesus. 'Everything is possible for
him who believes.' Immediately the boy's father exclaimed, 'I do
believe; help me overcome my unbelief!'"

Mark 9:21-24

Today's verse does not say everything but autism is possible
to overcome. It says EVERYTHING IS POSSIBLE. So, we
have it on good authority that autism can be overcome! God
already knows how to heal our kids. He doesn't have to figure
out how to do it. We must daily overcome our unbelief.

Because I was brought up in church and by Christian
parents, I never doubted God's ability to remove autism and
Neurofibromatosis from our son. My struggle with unbelief came in the form of questioning God; would He choose
to heal our son in my life time? My heart wavered when I
saw God's timing was not going to match my timing! In my
prayers I told God I knew He was able…but I questioned why
He was waiting to exercise His power. So many good things
are instilled in us when we learn to wait upon God.

I prayed for our son before he was conceived. I have
prayed for him everyday of his life. I took good care of myself
during pregnancy. We have laid hands on our son and prayed
many, many times. We have had pastors anoint him with oil
and lay hands on him to pray for his recovery. We have taken
our son to healing crusades, reached out our hands to the TV
when televangelist prayed and we have dropped to our knees
beside his bed many a late night. We have reached our arms
out to heaven and pleaded with God to show His mercies on

us. Our son's autism has lessened over the years, but our son is still autistic.

I still believe God will heal our son. I trust His timing no matter how long I must wait. I know deep in my heart God's timing is perfect. God is the Master of perfect order. Our nature is to be impatient and want the best for our children right now. When we do not know the "hows" and the "whys" it tends to frustrate us.

Today's verse links us with another parent. A parent who had a child with a difficult disorder. The parents response to Jesus was, "I do believe; help me overcome my unbelief." Today, make it your prayer to trust in Jesus and ask God to help you overcome any unbelief you might have.

Day #3

"Therefore we do not lose heart. Though outwardly we are wasting away, yet inwardly we are being renewed day by day. For our light and momentary troubles are achieving for us an eternal glory that far outweighs them all so we fix our eyes on not what is seen, but on what is unseen. For what is seen is temporary, but what is unseen is eternal."

II Corinthians 4:16-18

The Hebrew word for broken is shavar. This means, "to burst, break into pieces, wreck, crush, smash: tear into pieces (like a wild beast)…" Without a doubt, you and I have had our hearts broken when we learned of our children's diagnosis. Broken hearts lose hope, but only temporarily.

Today's verse reminds us if we don't renew our faith, after being broken hearted, we will waste away. To be renewed inwardly means we need to privately take care of our insides. This is done by reading Scripture and praying. If we stay broken hearted, we become very vulnerable.

We are Biblically instructed to not lose heart! This means we must put forth the effort to do research, improve our child's diet, continue to educate them and pray for them daily. All this is undoubtedly tiring. But when we are faithful and believe God at His word, the strength and the hope that is needed comes to us, and it will come to us on a daily basis.

An 'eternal glory' awaits each of us. To understand what this means we need to know what glory is. Glory means exalted honor, praise, a height of achievement. Our eternal glory will have something to do with what each of us goes through here on earth. So, if you handle raising a child with autism right…God is going to boast or brag about you for all of eternity!

For what is seen is 'temporary' means our child has a limited amount of time he/she has to live with autism. Eternal means having a beginning without an end; existing outside of time. Helping our child is preparing us for a higher service to do for all of eternity. What we are going through now will be outweighed by what is yet to come.

"Let us fix our eyes on not what we see," our child afflicted with autism. If we fix our eyes on what we see, we may lose heart. Our focus is to be on Jesus; the one who overcame death, the one who performs miracles, the one who knows what we do not yet know, and the one who sees what we do not see. Brokenness can lead to blessings from God. Know that future blessings will come from our current afflictions.

Today, tell God you don't want to lose heart. Ask Him to fix any part of your heart that is broken. Tell Him you will focus on Him and will choose to believe what affects your child now, is only temporary.

Day #4

"Then Jesus told his disciples a parable to show them that they should always pray and not give up. He said: 'In a certain town there was a judge who neither feared God nor cared about men. And there was a widow in that town who kept coming to him with the plea. Grant me justice against my adversary. For some time he refused. But finally he said to himself, "Even though I don't fear God or care about men, yet because this widow keeps bothering me, I will see that she gets justice so that she won't eventually wear me out with her coming!" And the Lord said, 'Listen to what the unjust judge says. And will not God bring about justice for His chosen ones, who cry out to Him day and night? Will He keep putting them off? I tell you, He will see that they get justice, and quickly. However, when the Son of Man comes, will He find faith on the earth?"'

Luke 18:1-8

Today's verses are a parable. A parable is defined as an earthly story with a heavenly meaning. Beyond the human story lies a truth with a spiritual lesson. Today's parable contains one simple truth: NEVER GIVE UP!

What a powerful parable for parents of children who need a healing touch from our God! We are to NEVER give up asking God to heal our children. I encourage you to wear God down with your petitions for your child! It is great to let God know our child is worth not giving up on. God can use this opportunity in our life to strengthen our prayer life with Him. I often find what God wants to do in me requires me to learn what I don't already know or do what I am not very good at doing!

If someone ever asks you when you are going to just stop searching for answers and accept your child for the way they are, you can say, "NEVER!" Tell them it is your job to keep praying and to continually ask God to heal your child completely. Today's parable will back you up! If you haven't been petitioning God on your child's behalf, it is never to late too start!

Today, in your prayers I want you to specifically name what your child needs. Cry out to God on behalf of your child! Be honest, sincere and let it be known that your child is worthy to have what he/she needs. God is listening.

Day #5

"He sent me to bind up the broken hearted."

Isaiah 61:1

Bind up means to tie up, secure, to hold up, or unite. So today we know Christ was sent from heaven to earth to hold us up. He came to unite us with him. It is good news that Jesus was sent to bind up the broken hearted. You and I had our hearts broken when we received our children's diagnosis. He brings us relief. Turning to Jesus is what starts the process of putting the pieces together.

Over the last seven years I have learned that autism is a battle. A battle that needs to be turned over to God. I need to hang onto God and let him lead…God always leads to victory. When I feel weary I am taking on too much of the battle myself; I need to step aside and turn it back over to God. Let Him fight for me. I do not need to spend my time fighting the enemy or seeking victory. I need to spend more of my time seeking Christ. As I bind myself to His presence and trust God…He will carry our son to victory.

We need to let God heal any brokenness that is still in our hearts. When we allow Jesus to do what God sent Him to do, gather us up and mend our brokenness, faith in God returns.

You and I are trusting God to heal our children in our lifetime. That requires faith. We will be blessed when God chooses to reward our faithfulness. Our children will reap the benefits of what we practiced and dared to believe.

Remember, this battle of autism is really for God to battle. God is raising up many leaders to discover answers about autism. God is leading many top notched doctors, scientists and researchers to answers and truths about this disorder. God is assembling brilliant people to take the heat, dig trenches and be bold in searching for a cure.

As God lifts us up and unites us all, we will not only see the healing begin, we will feel it. God is holding us up with His nail scared hands. I am sure you and I would just like God to heal our children through an instant miracle. But God is choosing most of us to walk the walk, talk the talk and learn the lesson of "walk by faith."

Today, spend some time memorizing the above verse. Think about how far God has already brought you and how your personal character is being challenged, molded and refined. God showed you His love by sending you His son to bind up your broken heart.

Day #6

"The mind of sinful man is death, but the mind controlled by the Spirit is for life and peace."

Romans 8:6

Peace means tranquility, serenity. How in the world does one get tranquility and serenity in a household that has an autistic child?! This seemed like such an oxy-moron to me!

In the early years our son's behaviors were very animalistic. When he ate a meal, food went everywhere! His behaviors could include: high pitched and loud screams, kicking, pinching, slamming doors, throwing things, banging his head against walls, biting us, self injury...the list was long. There was a time when my son couldn't pick me, his mother, out of a group of women. He did not know a thing about relationships. He only cared about someone meeting his needs.

I had to make a decision to fill my mind with Scripture. Yes, it is work and it took time. But if we do not fill our minds with Scripture, it becomes very easy to believe negative thoughts about our life with an autistic child. Life with a special needs child drains us financially, emotionally and even spiritually.

A sinful mind doesn't have to mean a mind is filled with pornography, addiction or adultery. A sinful mind can be a mind that has given up hope or a mind that is dwelling on negative thoughts. We must get on our knees and pray for the Holy Spirit to fill us. Pray for peace to be restored. God does not tear our mind down with negative thoughts, Satan does.

As we pray each of these 40 days, our relationship with God will grow stronger. When we draw closer to God, we get to know His heart. We see how big God's heart really is. We

learn to trust His greater purpose even when we don't understand why our child has autism.

When we change the way we think, God changes the way
we feel about our life and our child. Peace comes to us. Then
strength comes. Strength to do all we need to do to help our
precious children. Today I want you to get on your knees and
pray. Tell God you're sorry for the negative thoughts you've
had. Tell Him you're sorry for being angry at Him because
your child has autism. Tell Him you trust Him to help you
help your child overcome. Ask God to help you with your
thoughts today. Whenever you're willing to open up to God,
I promise He will listen to every word you say.

Day #7

> *"I pray that out of His glorious riches He may strengthen you with power through His Spirit in your inner being. So that Christ may dwell in your hearts through faith. And I pray that you being rooted and established in love, may have power, together with all the saints, to grasp how wide and long and high and deep is the love of Christ, and to know this love that surpasses knowledge, that you may be filled to the measure of all the fullness of God."*
>
> *Ephesians 3:16-19*

I started out asking for God to heal our son of autism. I still pray that prayer. But now I add to that prayer asking God to give me the strength and wisdom to raise our son. The Holy Spirit was given to us while Christ is in heaven. We can daily ask the Holy Spirit to be with us.

Autism came into our lives. God expects to be glorified with our testimony. It is an awesome thought to think God thinks so highly of our parenting skills! He knows we could handle this with His help…or He never would have allowed autism in.

Nothing we are doing or will do can cure our children of autism. God does all the healing. God gets the glory for our children's successes. Do you know God wants us to want Him and know Him MORE THAN He wants us to want healing for our child? I know how much I want our son healed…so that puts it in perspective for me how much God wants me to know Him.

Did you know that it is each of our jobs to know God intimately? That doesn't come by chance; it comes from study, prayer and worship. God deeply desires our involvement with Him. In fact we were created just for this purpose!

When I think how God lengthened my resume by adding: teacher, nurse, doctor, psychologist, occupational therapist, speech therapist, researcher, prayer warrior... I just chuckle! I am amazed at what I learned in the quest to help our son! The old saying, "there is no love like that of a mother for her child" is so true! Yet Christ's love for us is even deeper than the love we show our children. Imagine that. What Christ went through on the cross was the ultimate action of love.

Our children have taught us to love more deeply. Our children are teaching us to love like Christ loves. Our children are teaching us to never give up. Our children are teaching us love does indeed surpass knowledge.

Today, think about how much you love your child. Think about everything you have done to help your child. We help our children because we love them. We love our children because we know them. When we know God deeply, we love Him deeply too.

Day #8

"No eye has seen, no ear has heard, no mind has conceived what God has prepared for those who love Him." I Corinthians 2:9

The Hebrew word for prepare is hetolmazo. It refers to the spiritual blessings prepared by God for those of us that belong to Him. Imagine that, God is preparing a spiritual blessing for each of us!

Before you and I were born, God had a plan for each of us. He knew when I was a little girl I would grow up to be the mother of a child with autism. Our life now is part of the original plan.

God wants to do so much with the life of our children who have autism. We can't even imagine what is yet to come! You and I and our children are blessings, treasures to our God. He loves us! It is probably a good thing we are not seeing what He has in store for us. We would be overwhelmed if we knew what God already knows!

When I reflect on the theraies we have done, the money we have spent, the miles we have traveled to get help, the books I have read, the hours spent researching, the tutoring we have done in our home and realize all we have learned over the past seven years…I am nothing short of amazed. It is very clear to me that only because of God we have had enough stamina and resources to do all that has been done. My husband and I would be the first to say we are very glad that we did not know what lay ahead of us! We would have surely have checked out of this adventure had it been left up to us!

Our faith has been strengthened and our patience has been lengthened and we have dared to believe and take God at His word. God has already prepared our path, yours, mine and our children's. If this trial of raising a child with autism does not glorify God someday, then we are not letting God do a good work through us. Autism has a way of pointing out our weakness. Let us ask God today to make us strong in our weakness. He wants to do that for us. We just need to ask!

God has prepared a spiritual blessing for you and your child. Someday it will be revealed to you. Put it in your heart and in your mind that God loves you very much. He knows exactly what you are going through and He is here to help you. The plans He has for you and your child are very good and rewarding.

Today in your prayers ask God to strengthen you in the areas where you are weak. Tell Him you want to have a testimony for Him. Ask for the courage it takes to tell your testimony. Because you love God, tell Him you're looking forward to discovering the blessings He has in store for you!

Day #9

"We demolish arguments and every pretension that sets itself up against the knowledge of God, and we take captive every thought to make it obedient to Christ."

II Corinthians 10:5

Today's verse says we are to "demolish arguments…" this means to get a bulldozer or a wrecking ball and tear down our fears! We cannot meekly ask Satan to leave us and our children alone. We must make a firm stand with God to help our children.

We must get rid of the thoughts in our minds that tell us we cannot help our autistic children. Our children are just as valuable and loved by God as a normal developing child is. Our children need us to help them; they are unable to help themselves. That means we must not let Satan convince us that we are powerless to help our children. Satan always attacks us at our weakest points. He is the author of confusion.

Satan gave us an endless list to quit fighting for our son. Here is a few things that were on my list: We don't have enough money, we don't have the time that is required, how could I possibly quit my job and have our family live on one income? There is no local doctor that is willing to help me, we have no local school for us to put our son into, our son embarrasses me, I can't possibly home school – I am not a teacher, I am unqualified to be his parent, I am not the pioneering type… My list was pages long as to why I thought God picked the wrong mother to help our son.

God allowed our children to be afflicted by autism. That alone tells us this was God's plan. My parents told my husband and me, "God knows you can handle your son and his needs. God will help you to help Zack to overcome. God doesn't set you up to fail. If you fail, then God is not glorified and He has no testimony in you."

God wants people to turn to Him. He supplies the strength and He will meet our every need. Truth be known, Satan would love nothing more than to keep someone who loves God from having a testimony. Autism is awful in every definition of the word. But God allowed it to happen to our children. I trust that good will come out of this bad situation. I trust God to use each of our testimonies mightily.

I firmly believe every sacrifice that we make to do all we can for our children, is seen by God. Our efforts will return a blessing. We must press on. Take today's verse and make it your prayer today. Tell God of any fear, excuse or lie that you have in your heart. Don't let your mind hold you captive by anything that doesn't allow you to have hope or to move forward. After you tell God everything, focus on the thought that God still loves you and is with you in everything you do.

Day #10

"You will keep in perfect peace him whose mind is steadfast, because he trusts in you."

Isaiah 26:3

The word "keep" means to guard or shield. The word "steadfast" means fixed, unchanging, steady, firmly loyal and unswerving.

We must trust God with our heart and tell Him of the struggles we have with our kids. God already knows how we struggle in our minds with autism. But it is our job to put it into words and pray about it to Him. God promises to give us peace even though our mind wonders.

If we are going to be steadfast then we have to choose to believe the Bible, God's Word; and know it is the truth. God's mind does not wonder and does not doubt like our minds do. We must pray to Him and ask Him to be a watchman in our minds. God is capable of doing this and He wants to do this. He does not want Satan being the watchman in our minds.

When I find my mind thinking negative thoughts or dwelling on broken dreams, I make a conscience choice to stop. I quote Bible verses or put on Christian or uplifting music. I flood my mind with thoughts of God's power, God's love and hopeful words. I remind myself daily that nothing is too big for God to overcome. Not even autism.

I often remember what my parents said to me the night of our son's diagnosis. They said, "Always remember: The bigger the trial, the bigger God's testimony will be." I had to come to realize that just because the trial is bigger than me does not mean that the trial is too big for God.

You know, it would be a shame if we went through all that we are going through and we don't strengthen our character. We have been given an awesome opportunity to become more Christ like. Let's make the most of what we are going through. Your testimony may be wide spread or it may reach one other family that no one else can reach but you. If you tell God you want to have a testimony, He will make sure you have one for Him!

Satan is always hoping Christians will either be so ineffective we have no testimony or ruin the one we have. Choose to trust God. Fix your eyes and heart on Him. God will shield you and give you peace.

In your prayer today, tell God you want to have an effective testimony for Him. Tell Him you will give Him all you have and to make something for Him. When you offer God all you have, you will win His favor. Favor with God will change your life and the life of your child.

Day #11

"Blessed are you, O Israel! Who is like you, a people saved by the Lord? He is your shield and helper and your glorious sword. Your enemies will cower before you, and you will trample down their high places."

Deuteronomy 33: 29

A shield is a defensive weapon of war. Yahweh is another name for God. In today's verse God was being a shield for his people.

The pain that came to our hearts when our son was diagnosed with autism was so strong it captivated my mind for about one and a half years. We are held captive by anything that keeps us from living the life God wants for us. I was captivated because it paralyzed me from moving forward. Autism not only invaded our son, it invaded our entire family, our entire life. It wreaked havoc with our finances, our time, our home, our friendships, our jobs…in fact it is so pervasive, there was not any part of our lives which it did not affect. In many ways, Satan won for a while.

Our prayers seemed to go unanswered and unheard. It was a daily struggle to live with a child who seemed animalistic in the early years, he seemed unreachable and the burden weighed very heavy on us. We prayed to God to strip Satan of the power he had on our son. We asked God to control our thoughts, restore our hope and remove us from denial. We had to put God back in the 'high places' in our minds. It has to be a conscience prayer to put God back in charge of our lives.

We prayed continually, minute by minute, hour by hour, day by day…it was that bad. It was time to make Satan cower before God and trample down the high place that we had allowed him to have in our lives.

Once we had enough of Satan, we saturated ourselves by reading, researching and going into deeper prayers. My husband and I made a conscience effort to stop dwelling on all the negative. In our cars and in our home, we only listened to positive, uplifting music. That brought hope for a new day.

Blessings will come if we get back to studying God's Word every day. In the midst of a chaotic life, we have to get back to a place where we find time for God. We need to walk with God, not God walk with us. In today's prayer let us say, "Lord, let me walk with God, not God walk with me. I will not ask God to bless what I do today. I will do what He leads me to do and He will bless me. Amen."

Day #12

"If any man builds on this foundation using gold, silver, costly stones, wood, hay or straw, his work will be shown for what it is, because the Day will bring it to light. It will be revealed with fire, and the fire will test the quality of each man's work." I Corinthians 3:12-13

There are two judgments we face as a Christian. In the first judgment we will be asked if we accepted Christ as our Lord and Savior. This judgment will allow us to enter the gates of heaven or send us directly to hell. The second judgment comes to judge our works. What did we do with our time on earth? Things done that were meaningless will burn up like wood, hay and straw when put to the fire. Things that were done of value will stand the test of fire. Gold, silver and costly stones will stand the test of fire.

I believe working with our kids and all that it entails is gold, silver and costly stones. When our works are put before us in heaven, the time that we have spent cooking meals from scratch, tutoring our children, spending our money on their needs, the struggles that it took to get them to take the supplements their bodies needed, spending sleepless nights reading and researching to help them will all stand the test of the fire that is yet to come.

How mad have you gotten because your child has autism? I pray that we come through this trial with a better character than when each of us started. I pray Satan is shocked at the fight we put up to help save our children.

Satan came to steal, kill and destroy. Look around, he is succeeding in a lot of families these days. I plan to take our son back and walk away with more than I started with! God wants to teach us, expand us and repay us for our losses. God and God alone equips us for the battle we are in with our children.

Take an assessment of the foundation you are building on. Make sure your heart is right with God. One day we all will stand before God and our works will go through the fire. We don't want to end up with a pile of ashes. When we know better, we do better.

Spend time today with your child. Love your child. Find a way to help your child. Pray for your child. Your hard work and prayers will stand the second judgment of fire. You, my dear parent, will not end up with a pile of ashes. You will end up with a foundation of gold, silver and costly stones! I pray each of us comes through this trial stronger than we ever would have imagined. Knowing when we are weak, God is strong.

Day #13

This is what the Lord says – your Redeemer, the Holy One of Israel. "I am the Lord your God, who teaches you what is best for you, who directs you in the way you should go."

Isaiah 48:17

The word "redeemer" means rescuer or deliverer. That means Christ is our redeemer. He is the one who rescues or the One who will deliver us. We need to know who Christ is. After all, we're asking Him to rescue and deliver our children from autism. Spending time reading our Bible and praying will help us to know who Jesus is.

God does not make mistakes. As hard as it is to believe, our children have autism for a reason. God will direct our paths if we seek Him. How does God direct our path anyway? He leads us to books to read, He puts a helpful parent in our path, or He may quicken our heart to know when something is right or wrong.

Jesus Christ lived life without sin. His body was a blood sacrifice on a cross. All of our sins – every person of every generation – were heaped upon His broken and bruised body. He conquered death when He arose on the third day. He is in heaven now with God. One day, soon, returning for those who love Him. That is who Jesus is. This is the one who is teaching us and directing our paths.

I cringed when I realized that our son having autism is 'what is best' for me. But God in all of His wisdom knew this is the path I should travel. It will strengthen me, challenge me and bring the most glory to Him. This path is paved with tears and prayers. It is a path that has brought many wonderful people in our lives that I would not have otherwise met. My Lord is teaching me to know Him better and to trust Him more.

So, why are our children afflicted? I do not know. How long will they be afflicted? I do not know. Why are some kids recovering from autism and not others? I do not know. There are endless questions we all have that are all answered with, "I do not know."

So let us focus on what we do know today! God is our teacher. He knows what is best for us, and our children. God will direct us on what to do to help our children…if we seek Him. God knows our situation and He is working 24/7 in ways we do not yet know. God doesn't make mistakes. God is in control.

You have taken a very good step in letting God teach you. You have committed to 40 consecutive days of at least reading and praying. Be assured, God is directing your paths. Today I want you to think about Jesus being your Redeemer. Ask Him to direct your path. He'll put you on a path that is best for you.

Day #14

For I know the plans I have for you, "declares the Lord, plans to prosper you and not to harm you, plans to give you hope and a future. Then you will call upon Me and come and pray to Me, and I will listen to you. You will seek Me and find Me when you seek Me with all your heart."

Jeremiah 29:11-12

These are my favorite verses in the Bible when I think of our son. Oh, how my heart needs to know that God has a plan to prosper our son. A plan that includes hope and a future! It is a promise I have deep in my heart and think about everyday!

Early on I decided to put my heart on the line and hope and pray for a full recovery from autism for our son. I do not know God's plan for our son. But I do know our son is a child of God. I know I can trust God's judgment and rely on His wisdom. If I can believe God's holy Word, then I have to believe He has a plan for our son. This plan includes a future. A future that will glorify God. Whatever God's plan is, it is perfect. No more, no less. Today's verse can restore our hope. Even though we can sometimes feel completely blind to what the future will be, we still need to press forward.

I think of how my husband and I plan a new vacation to take our kids on. My husband and I have it all planned out. We know the way, the cost, the activities and the outcome. But our children know none of this. They must trust us that we know what we are doing. As the parents we know the roads we will take to get there, we know where we are taking them and yet our children must trust we will bring them home safely and with good memories.

Think of this autism journey in the same way. Our heavenly Father knows the way, the cost, the activities and the outcome. He even knows that we will get through this journey safely and with some happy memories!

Jeremiah 29:11 tells us God has a plan but verse 12 tells us we need to do our part. To go, pray and talk with God and this must be done with ALL of our hearts.

God wants quiet undisturbed time with us. For us to give Him all of our heart means we have to be serious about our prayer time. Time spent praying, reading and singing praise songs to Him.

Trusting God completely means trusting that if He has allowed something so difficult to happen to one of His children, He plans to use it mightily if we will let Him. Today's verse is God's promise to you, me and our children. God's unseen, unknown plan is the perfect plan and just because we don't see or know the plan, does not mean God doesn't have the perfect plan.

Today, I challenge you to memorize Jeremiah 29:11-12. Write it on a sticky note and put it in your car, on your bathroom mirror or anywhere else you will see it several times during the day. Personalize the verses by putting your child's name wherever the word 'you' is in verse 11.

Day #15

"Let us not become weary in doing good, for at the proper time we will reap a harvest if we do not give up. Therefore, as we have opportunity, let us do good to all people, especially to those who belong to the family of believers."

Galatians 6:9-10

The word "weary" means to become exhausted, to tire oneself, to faint, lose heart or to give up. Christ is telling us here when we are doing the right things, not to let ourselves get weary.

Easier said than done, right?! I do get weary! Here I am, in my own corner of the world, cooking every morsel of food that goes into our son's mouth from scratch. Home schooling him many hours a day. I give our son supplement after supplement several times a day. I take him to several therapies every week. Not to mention making regular phone consultations with doctors and researching on the computer and reading countless books to find ways to help him…my head just spins! All the while, I am raising two other children and keeping my marriage in tact!

By doing all we can for our children, we are doing right. The work we do on our children's behalf is our seed. If we don't plant seeds for our children, then there is no seed for God to multiply. We are in the right place at the right time, whether we like it or not!

I once took our son to a local speech therapist. He evaluated our son and asked me about what I was doing at home. When I explained the intensive ABA schooling that we were doing at the time, the diet we have him on, the supplements we give him and the research we were still doing, the therapist looked at me in astonishment. He said to me, "You know, Kathy, you can't do everything that you are doing and not succeed. It will break open and you will get results when the time is right." I will never forget those words. He was right, when God says the time is right, all things will come together and we'll be fine. God will bring forth a harvest in due time. We just have to keep on pressing forward.

The second part of Galatians 6:9 says, "…for at the proper time we will reap a harvest if we do not give up." I live in an agricultural valley. I see farmers plant their seeds and in a predictable time, a harvest is reaped. Never in the same season is the harvest reaped as when the seed is sown. You have a season all of its own to plant. And we will have our own season to reap the harvest.

Our children need our help. They cannot help themselves. God gave each of us our children. A child that complements us and our families. We must not grow weary of helping our children. They need us and we need them. If you are tired, rest but do not give up. The harvest is forth coming!

In your prayers today, tell God if you are tired and why. Then, tell Him you will continue to plant seeds so your child can reap the harvest someday. Promise to not give up even if you get weary.

Day #16

"...for I have learned to be content whatever the circumstances. I know what it is to be in need, and I know what it is to have plenty. I have learned the secret of being content in any and every situation, whether living in plenty or in want. I can do everything through him who gives me strength." Philippians 4:11-13

Philippians 4:13 is a verse near and dear to my heart. This was probably one of the first verses I ever memorized. My parents instilled in me from a young age there was nothing I couldn't achieve with God's help. It is a verse we need to have memorized as parents of autistic children. It was much harder to implement the previous verse where Paul talks about being content here and now. It is what God wants from us: To be content and accepting of our children while they are still afflicted with autism.

The human nature in us gets angry, questions why, how and when will all of this come to an end. Only God knows the answers to those tough questions. But it is possible to be content while we are on this journey. It takes prayer. Asking God to help us, lead us, teach us and show us His way.

Paul had to learn to be content. We must also learn to be content. Being content means to be satisfied. We can search for answers and still learn to be grateful for where we are at any given time.

If we rely on our own strength, we find we quickly run out of strength. So what does it mean to, "do everything through him..."? It means to pray for wisdom and direction. If we run out of words when we pray, then it is time to pray for a prayer language. A prayer language is when we pray words we don't understand. Like a foreign language. When we pray in a prayer language the Holy Spirit intercedes with new words, new prayers.

I often use my prayer language in my quiet prayers to God. This gives me a sense of peace to know the Holy Spirit has new words for my same old prayers. Learning to be content in our situation is an ongoing lesson. We know what it is like to be in need. Let's pray and ask Jesus to give us the daily dose of strength we need.

Today, ask God to help you be content with where your child is now. If your prayers sound the same day after day, night after night, then ask the Holy Spirit to come and give you your very own prayer language. I promise, He'll never run out of words when He intercedes for you.

Day #17

"For the eyes of the Lord are on the righteous and His ears are attentive to their prayer, but the face of the Lord is against those who do evil."

1 Peter 3:12

Attentive means paying attention, observant, listening or devoted. God is listening to the prayers of His children and today's verse promises His ears are attentive to our prayers. Is God taking care of those of us who are already saved and is He hearing our prayers? Yes! One thing I really believe is God does not minimize how much autism breaks the hearts of the parents. God cares about the physical, emotional, mental and spiritual sides of our children. Everything that concerns us, concerns God. Jesus came to free our kids. Jesus came to mend our broken hearts.

God wants us to be successful. If He doesn't help us, to help our children, then we don't have a testimony for Him. If we don't have a testimony, He will not be glorified. God has not turned a deaf ear to our prayers. God still does miracles today. I think there is a purpose for taking the long road to recovery from autism. It builds our character to be more Christ like. It makes us seek out God and it allows people to take notice when we do something so hard, for so long, in the right way. We may not like God taking us down the long hard road. But God is going to do what it takes for us to build our character and glorify Him.

I like watching caterpillars. They are very low to the ground. They move slowly. It takes them a long time to get anywhere. You don't hear them like you hear a bird. There seems to be no voice in them. Then one day, they wrap them- selves up in a silk cocoon, sometimes hanging only by a thread.

For two days they rock their heads back and forth to release silk from their body. They stay in a dark, warm unassuming place. Within a very confined space, they morph their bodies into a beautiful butterfly! Soon, it emerges and bears no resemblance of its former self: The same being but in a different form. Its colors are bright and rich in color. It no longer crawls...it flies!!!

It has been a prayer of mine for our son to someday talk, socialize with others and worship our God! I want our son to tell others what God did for him. For in many ways he is our little caterpillar and we are his cocoon. May God answer the prayers of mothers and fathers and give our children the ability to someday fly. For if you're like me, you have a thousand dreams still to be realized for your child.

Today's verse is a promise to parents that God's eyes are watching and His ears are attentive to our prayers. In your prayers today be very aware of God looking straight at you and He is more than listening to your prayers. He is completely devoted to you.

Day #18

"For God did not give us a spirit of timidity, but a spirit of power, of love and of self-discipline."

2 Timothy 1:7

Timidity means fearful. Fear is not of God. It is easy to have fear when you have a child that self-injures, cannot follow directions, tantrums in unbelievable ways, cannot talk and fears people. Fear of the future, fear of not being able to handle what we've been given to handle, fear of the unknown, these are just a few things we have each had to deal with. Please know that when we have fear, it is clearly not sent by God. God does not want us to have fear. When fear is riding high in our life, we need to pray.

Pray and tell God we need to feel His love. Pray for the Holy Spirit to come and fill us. Some days, we need to fill our mind with Christian music, old hymns or catchy choruses. Sometimes when I feel fear overcoming me, I make visual pictures in my mind. I picture myself laying my fears down at the foot of the cross. I might visualize myself sitting on a log next to a stream talking with Jesus. These kinds of exercises can really help.

If fear is not from God, then where does it come from? The answer is Satan. When we pray to God to help us overcome our fears, God answers. He sends the Holy Spirit to fill us with His love. With love comes the ability to have self-discipline. With self-discipline comes power: Power to forge through another day, Power to help our children, Power to keep on searching for solutions to our children's needs.

Satan would rather we do anything but pray. He knows God listens to the prayers of His children. Prayer gives us understanding and power. Some of the greatest truths we will ever learn are learned through praying.

My father has often said there will be rewards in heaven that will be handed out to mothers and fathers for being constant prayer warriors for their children. Prayer is such a personal, unseen heroic, selfless task. If we never knew how to pray before, our children get the credit for developing this gift in us!

In your prayer time today, visualize yourself laying your fears at the foot of the cross. Visualize yourself talking with Jesus. Talk with Him like you would talk with your best friend.

Day #19

"Come to me, all you who are weary and burdened, and I will give you rest. Take my yoke upon you and learn from me, for I am gentle and humble in heart, and you will find rest for your souls. For my yoke is easy and my burden is light." Matthew 11:28-30

Our load is heavy and it is easy to get weary. But it is not impossible to bear, with the help of Jesus. We were not designed to handle autism on our own. There are days, when it is best if we back down, take a breather and just rest in God's arms.

The word "rest" means refreshment, relief. In the old days when they yoked two oxen together, it was a strong ox and a weak ox that were yoked together. With harnesses around each of their necks, they were held together and this allowed the weaker ox not to stray or fall. The stronger ox guided and carried the weaker ox. We are no different. We are to be yoked with Christ. He will guide us. He will carry us. He will lead us. But we must be yoked with Him for this to happen. When we yoke ourselves to God, we cannot help but learn from Him.

Today's verse tells us when we yoke ourselves to Christ; we will find rest for our souls. I often find it is my soul that needs the rest more than my actual physical body does. My soul is what I put on the line for our son. My soul is what is interceding in prayers. My soul is my spiritual and emotional part of me that is so vested in helping our son be who God designed him to be. My soul finds its rest when I yoke myself to Jesus Christ.

How do we yoke ourselves to Jesus? We do this by spending time in prayer, reading our bible, talking with God throughout our day, good days and bad days, doing studies like you are doing right now, telling God everything; every little detail. From the frustrations of changing dirty underwear for the umpteenth time to the frustration of being pinched for the millionth time and all the way to the joys of hearing the words, "Mommy, I love you."

If you're tired, yoke yourself to Jesus. He will give you rest. Rest your soul. There's an old saying, "he who suffers most, has the most to give." We go through a lot day in and day out. Most people have no idea what it's like to walk in our shoes. We will have a lot to offer others when God brings us through. Yoke yourself with Christ and get the rest you so need and deserve.

Today, I want you to do something for yourself. Give yourself permission to pamper yourself. Treat yourself to something that will give you some rest and bring a smile to your face.

Day #20

"And the God of all grace, who called you to his eternal glory, in Christ, after you have suffered for a little while will Himself restore you and make you strong, firm and steadfast!"

I Peter 5:10

I have learned over the years God is a God of grace. What is grace anyway? Grace is favor. The dictionary describes grace as "A disposition to be generous, helpful or good will. A favor rendered by one who needs not do so, indulgence. Divine love and protection bestowed freely upon mankind." This is who the God we serve is. This is His personality. The One we will spend eternity with. Wow!

Today's verse teaches us that our God is helpful, gives us undeserved favor, indulges us, protects us and has a divine love for all of mankind. Knowing this will help us to forge through our daily struggles helping us with our children. God gives grace freely and unconditionally, even when we don't deserve it.

A day with the Lord is like a thousand years to us. So, when Peter says, "…after you have suffered for a little while…" this means that suffering can last for years in our time frame!!! But do not be discouraged my dear friend, Peter also says God "…Himself will restore us and make us strong, firm and steadfast!" Who is going to make us strong, firm and steadfast? God. Not a friend, not our spouse, not an angel but God Himself.

Whenever I mumble of the pain or energy that it takes to do something, my husband will often say, "No pain, no gain!" Well, on a hard day I gain miles in this marathon race of pulling our son out of the pit of autism!

God indulges us, loves us and protects us. Have you ever been away from your kids and upon returning they tackle you as you come through the door? Usually saying, "Glad your back, what did you bring me?" While you were out you thought of them, individually and you bought just the right surprise for each of them. It makes you happy to make them happy. Well, God is thinking of you. You have not been forgotten. God has blessings to give to you. You have been called to His eternal glory.

There is no end to eternity. Our God wants us to spend all of eternity with Him. He has favor to give us, and I bet He can't wait! Today, dwell upon the fact it is God, and God alone, who is restoring you, making you strong, firm and steadfast. It is God who is calling you to bring glory to Him.

Day #21

"Let the Peace of Christ rule in your hearts, since as members of one body you were called to peace. And be thankful." Colossians
3:15

The Hebrew word for peace is shalom. It means, a sense of tranquility, or a state of calm without anxiety or stress. Peace from Christ is unique in that it is everlasting and flawless, unlike any peace offered by the world.

Raising a child with autism can be stressful and turn a peaceful home into a chaotic household in no time flat! We learned early on that we could not raise our voices or spank any of our children because it upset our son who has autism. If we did, our son cried uncontrollably for two hours! It made a bad situation worse. Our son is so in tune to tones of voices it made us consciously decide to stay calm and collected in times when we would normally get mad. It took less effort to stay in control than it did to calm him down when he was scared or upset.

For a long time, my husband was upset that he could not do a human natured response like get mad. We all have a right to get mad, and that is true. But how do we handle our anger? My husband and I had to work on staying calm like we thought Christ would do in our situation. It was no easy task. The hardest days came when we were tired and didn't get enough sleep the night before. If we didn't stay calm, our son would cry. Sometimes he would get so worked up he would try to injure himself or attack me. He could not and still to this day cannot stand to see anyone get yelled at.

Learning to stay calm, not to raise our voices took a lot of work....and God gave us plenty of times to practice it! It is now a rare occasion that the peace in our home is disrupted. Because we are sinful people, I cannot say we never get mad.

Far from it! But we have learned to think and not react first. We have a peaceful home. More peaceful and calm, I would say, than the average American family! Only God can help those of us who have families with an autistic child to have a peaceful home.

This is a lesson learned fully and truly only because our son could not handle not having peace and calmness in our home! I am thankful for such a hard lesson learned. When we have such lessons, today's verse reminds us to be thankful. Today, pray and ask God to help you stay calm. Ask God to help you not to over react to a bad situation. Pray for peace and calm to fill your home. Remember to be thankful for what God has given you, what He's done for you and for what He is yet to do for you and your child!

Day #22

"No temptation has seized you except what is common to man. And God is faithful: He will not let you be tempted beyond what you can bare. But when you are tempted, He will also provide a way out so that you can stand up under it." 1 Corinthians 10:13

The word temptation means trial. Seized means overtaken. Faithful means trustworthy, dependable and reliable. Bare means to endure or resist. Way out means a way of escape. Stand up means to endure.

We must press on. It would do no good to quit this fight. We cannot leave our children in the place they are in. Early on, I was sure autism could destroy me. It is so pervasive. It affects my child's mind, body and our entire family and it reached into every area of our lives. I definitely thought this was more than I could handle. More than we could handle as a family. But guess what? It hasn't destroyed us. It hasn't ripped our lives apart to the point of breaking our family up. We have learned what God's unfailing love really is.

We are not fighting this battle alone by any stretch of the imagination. We have gotten emotional and financial support from grandparents, friends and our church. We have stayed in tune to God's plan for our lives by reading, praying and pressing on every day.

Believing God is faithful is a choice. I chose to believe God at His word. I love Mother Teresa's saying, "I know that God won't give me anything more than I can handle. I just wish He didn't trust me so much!" Wow, what does God know about each of us that we don't know about ourselves? Now there is a thought to ponder!

Our trial is helping our children to overcome autism. Our children have a body and a mind that has been overtaken by a disorder called autism. God is trustworthy, dependable and reliable. We are to endure our situation. God will undoubtedly provide a way of escape. We must endure.

God does provide us help. Help comes by consulting with a DAN (Defeat Autism Now!) doctor, reading books, implementing dietary changes in our kids. Is all this work? Yes, but it does provide noticeable results for our children. Today's verse tells us God will show us ways to endure what we are going through. God is here with us and he is faithful.

When you pray today, thank God. Thank Him for showing you ways to help your child. Thank Him for being faithful. Thank Him that your child is on the road to recovery.

Day #23

"Jesus looked at them and said, 'With man this is impossible, but with God all things are possible.'"

Matthew 19:26

Do I believe God can heal a child with autism? Yes. That takes no faith for me. The faith for me comes in the form of believing God will heal our son in my lifetime. It is not if God can heal, it is, when is God going to heal our son? God has His timing and His reasons for waiting. I could not possibly make autism go away no matter what I choose to do for our son. It would be impossible for me. But autism going away in our children is totally possible for our loving and wonderful God. The meaning of possible means it is capable of happening.

I think we can believe in Christ for our salvation in a matter of seconds and yet we spend the rest of our life believing in Him for little more. Having a child with such severe needs strips us of many layers and gets to the core of what we believe. There are times when I just want to be told the truth and nothing more.

I can look at my bookshelves filled with books on autism. A wealth of information at my finger tips about the disorder. Books on those who have recovered children, books on diet, books on supplements and books on bio medical jargon that makes my head spin. I have read them all and still wonder what I know for sure! We have a lot of information on autism today and yet many questions go unanswered.

I have many days where I choose not to read about autism. I chose to just read the Bible. There are days when we just need the break from reading about interventions for autism. When we read the Bible, we fill our head, heart and spirit with God's truths. Truths that all things are possible with God.

I once read an interesting fact about bumble bees.

Their wing span is not proportional to their body size. Aerodynamically it is impossible for a bumble bee to fly. But bumble bees have no idea they are not built to fly, so they fly. This is just one example of the impossible happening everyday. It reminds us when God designs it, anything is possible! Every time I look at a bumble bee, I smile and it reminds me God has the ultimate say. I hope that you never look at a bumble bee the same again! Look at it and smile. Remember that God designed our children after His own image. God will have the ultimate say.

Today when you pray, tell God you know it is not impossible for Him to heal your child, completely. Tell Him you will have faith that He is going to heal your child in your lifetime.

Day #24

"They spit on him, and took the staff and struck him on the head again and again…then they lead him away to crucify him."
Matthew 27:30, 31

I remember watching the movie "The Passion of Christ" by Mel Gibson. When they had Christ tied in the courtyard and whipped his back repeatedly, I remember crying. As I closed my eyes and heard the whip crack, I knew flesh was flying in the air. I whispered, "That one is for autism." Then the whip was drawn back and seconds later there was another crack of the whip. More skin left my precious Savior's back. More blood was shed. "That one is for Neurofibromatosis," I whispered.

Then and there it confirmed the fact that Christ took it upon His body for what our son was now suffering for. We have full victory over autism. Christ paid the price, He suffered and the battle is His.

The cross is so important to us Christians. Many times when I pray I picture myself kneeling at the foot of the cross and laying down whatever is burdening me. Every fear, every question, every new therapy. I take it to the cross. I pray to be given wisdom and for God's answers to be clear to me.

The cross is a symbol of hope to us Christians. Jesus died on a cross. His death and resurrection accomplished what no other religion could. It bridged the gap between us and God. Is your heart aching for your child to be healed? Is worry stealing your sleep? Do you long for your child to have a friend? Do you worry about the money it takes to get your child treatments? Take every prayer and lay it at the cross.

Christ, the Son of God, came from heaven to earth. He lived His life blamelessly for thirty-three years. His body was the sacrifice to reconcile you and me to our God. Jesus' blood was pure, untainted. This is what is meant by the term "covered by the blood." Only the best was chosen for a sacrifice. Once we were sinners, God had to have His Son pay the bloody sacrifice for us to reconcile with God. Once we understand the price has been paid for our lives, it becomes easier to have faith.

God is good. He is our anchor. He cares for you, me and our children. We must continue to trust in Him. We must submit ourselves to God's hands. God may use doctors and scientists to give us clues or answers about our kids. But it is Jesus who holds the key to our children overcoming autism.

We need to stand steadfast. Push forward. Continue to drop to our knees. When our prayers go up, God will send His blessings. Trials like what we are going through are what separate the weak from the strong. Today, think about Christ being crucified. My dear parent, Christ took the beating, let's claim our promise and remember He is faithful to those who trust Him.

Day #25

"No, in all these things we are more than conquerors through Him who loved us."

Romans 8:37

Conquer in the dictionary is described as, "to defeat or subdue by force. To overcome or surmount by physical, mental or moral force. To win." The pain we feel because of autism is inevitable. But staying miserable and hanging onto broken dreams is optional.

Are we supposed to be afraid of autism? No, the Bible promises God will not give us more than we are able to handle. The key to the above verse is, "…through Him…" On our own we cannot conquer autism. Jesus Christ supplies the strength, the wisdom and the love we need on a daily basis with our children. On my own, I can get overwhelmed, exhausted, scared, hurt and angry.

You don't set out to climb a mountain and then half way up say that you have conquered the mountain. That mountain is not conquered until you are at the top! Autism is conquered when our children are talking, thinking and behaving like we imagined they would do, when they were still in our womb.

I don't know about you, but I am looking for a future that is autism and Neurofibromatosis free for our son!!! Anything short of a complete recovery is not what we are praying for. If we are to "…conquer" through Christ, then that is a promise of a complete recovery.

Love. Where do we get the love needed to help our children? Some days it comes easily. Other days, it is honestly a struggle. Not because of the child. But because of the behaviors or lack of skills. Still, if Christ can love each of us…then we can love our children.

Christ loved each of us enough to die for us when we

were not worthy. The example for how we are to love was set then and there. Everyone is worthy to be loved. Our kids are worth every ounce of effort, strength and nickel that it takes from us. Today's verse tells us we can win this battle we are fighting, with God's help. Don't give up; this battle will be won in the end.

Today, visualize your child overcoming all he/she needs to overcome. Don't short change your child by accepting anything short of a full recovery. Tell God you know this victory will come because of Him.

Day #26

*"To keep me from becoming conceited because of those surpass-
ingly great revelations, there was given me a thorn in my flesh,
a messenger of Satan, to torment me. Three times I pleaded with
the Lord to take it away from me. But He said to me, "My grace
is sufficient for you, for my power is made perfect in weakness."*
II Corinthians 12:7-9

Sufficient in the dictionary means, "as much as needed,
enough, adequate."

Paul wrote of his vision and of his physical pain in his
flesh. He said his thorn in his flesh was of Satan and that
Satan tormented him with it. Though we do not know what
the thorn was, Paul says God's grace was sufficient.

Autism is the thorn in my flesh. If God's grace is sufficient
for us then that means we get as much grace as we need! I
don't know about you, but I am as ordinary as anyone! I don't
possess the gift of teaching a special needs child. I don't natu-
rally possess patience and I surely don't possess any knowledge
on how to find a cure for autism! But the above verse promises
me God's power is manifested in my weakness.

God uses the ordinary. I think by using ordinary people,
the testimony is more powerful. Most of us are ordinary...are
we not? Ordinary people are easy to identify with. Ordinary
people remove the excuses that we like to hide behind.

Autism can seem so permanent if you listen to the wrong
people. Since we deal with it day in and day out, it can be
easy to lose sight of that, which God wants us to overcome.
I believe God's purpose for our children suffering is greater
than our immediate discomfort. We want healing now but we
must believe that waiting longer for our healing to come will
bring greater glory to God.

God wants us to learn to trust Him. Trust requires time.

It requires patience. It requires suffering. We need to be so desperate, that we turn to God and God alone.

Today's verse reminds us that God's grace is all we need to get through our day. We have been given enough grace to handle anything that comes our way. We have no reason to feel overwhelmed or stressed out. When you pray today, realize that God will give you as much grace as you need. He will manifest His power in your weakness.

Day #27

"Show me Your ways, O Lord, teach me Your paths; guide me in Your truth and teach me, for You are God my Savior, and my hope is in You all day long."

Psalm 25:5

"Show me your ways, O Lord" means we want God to "bring to light" or "reveal" to us the way He wants us to go. Hope means expectation. The word guide in today's verse means to lead, explain or instruct. This is exactly what we want from God. We want Him to lead us. Instruct us and to reveal to us what He wants us to do for our children. I need the truth to be told to me. I need to be taught what I do not know. I want to be open to learning more. All my expectations are put in Christ.

Just having faith is pointless. Our faith has to be based on Jesus overcoming death. It is our faith in Jesus Christ that moves God. Jesus is to be our foundation for having faith that our children will overcome autism. If you know what is going to happen, then that is not faith! Faith in God will move mountains. When we read Scripture, we can relate it to our situation. We can claim its promises persistently in our prayers until God keeps His word.

I don't see much on the news that offers hope for a cure to autism. Yet through many computer networks and conferences I see hope for a cure abound. When people push through fear, doubt and other obstacles, great things happen. Determination, driven by love for a child, always brings results. We must seek out what we do not yet know. Blessings will come.

I have noticed when I get the courage to believe or try something it doesn't take long for doubt to set in. My courage starts being melted away by the fear that comes into my mind.

Isn't that just like the devil?! Using fear to melt away our courage. That is why we need to pray and ask God to show us His truths, to teach us what we need to know. When we pray and ask, God always comes through.

Ask God to show you His ways, to teach you His ways, to show you His truth and to restore your hope. God is great at making a way when there is no way. Let today's verse be your prayer. Let's make our stumbling blocks become stepping stones for our children to cross over! Pray and ask God to make you strong in the areas you are weak.

Day #28

"The Lord is the everlasting God, the Creator of the ends of the earth. He will not grow tired or weary, and His understanding no one can fathom. He gives strength to the weary and increases the power of the weak. Even youths grow tired and weary, and young men stumble and fall; but those who hope in the Lord will renew their strength. They will soar on wings like eagles; they will run and not grow weary, they will walk and not be faint."

Isaiah 40:28-31

Millerton Lake is a local lake where I live. Every January and February people get on boats to cruise the lake to watch the local eagles fly. The eagles are easy to spot and beautiful to watch. Our eagles will flock to Canada at the end of February.

When there is a storm that comes, an eagle will leave the security of its nest and spread its wings to ride the air currents of the approaching storm. They instinctively know the air currents of a storm will carry it higher in the sky than it could ever soar on its own. Eagles never flock together. When you look for an eagle you look for them one at a time and you have to look up high to find one.

When I think of a bird soaring I don't think they get tired. The winds are carrying them. Flapping there wings constantly would be the action that tires them out. To soar and not have to work at flying must feel so incredible. It's probably the best part of being a bird!

Turkeys are a whole different kind of bird! A turkey will hide during a storm. They would never dare to leave a barn when a storm comes. They stay covered and wait for storms to pass. Guess what? We are in a storm. The storm of autism. Which kind of bird will we be like? The eagle or the turkey?

Let us spread our wings and put our faith and trust in Jesus. We need to face this storm head on and rise above its nastiness. Maybe then we can feel what it feels like to fly without flapping our wings so hard! Let's ask Jesus not only to carry us but to teach us how to soar like an eagle! The Bible promises if we soar like an eagle, we can run and not grow weary. We can walk and will not feel faint. What a neat promise we have today!

When you pray today, tell God you long to soar above the storm of autism. Ask Him to be the wind that takes you higher. Put more of your hope in the Lord today. He will renew your strength.

Day #29

"Those who sow in tears will reap with songs of joy. He who goes out weeping, carrying seed to sow, will return with songs of joy, carrying sheaves with Him."

Psalm 126:5-6

I cannot count the days I went into our tutor room and cried all the while I tutored our son! I did not tutor because I wanted to tutor. In fact there were days I didn't even want to be around our son. I tutored because God wanted me to tutor. It was His choice for me to teach our son, not mine!

How did I know it was God's choice for me to quit my paying job and stay home and teach our son? Because, I know God gave me each of our children. One of them is just not able to talk, socialize or take care of himself. I couldn't deny our child of the potential that I know is somewhere in him.

I was a life insurance agent for fifteen years prior to quitting and staying home to raise and home school our son. The amount of money I earned working could help to cover the cost of so many therapies. We needed money for so many new costs. Costs of supplements, speech therapy, occupational therapies, new books that I need to read, seminars that I wanted to attend, out of area doctor fees and special food that I needed to buy to feed our son. So why was I going to stop that stream of income? I had a very hard time controlling our child, because he had animalistic behaviors in the early years. I felt God wanted me around our son more than He wanted anyone else around him. No one could read and understand this child as well as I could, and I didn't always do the best job! So, I went to the tutor room and gave it my best shot! Praying God would take my best efforts as seeds that were being planted in fertile ground.

Living in an agricultural valley, I knew a little bit about

farming. This is what I knew. Seeds that were not planted in fertile ground did not grow. Seeds that are not watered do not grow. Seeds planted are never harvested in the same season that they are planted. A season or two needs to go by before fruits of one's labor are realized. When I got done tutoring our son, I would leave the tutor room and know I was one day closer to him recovering from autism. How many days would all this take, I did not know. Six years later, I still don't know the answer to that question.

What I do know is God never gives us a trial so big that it can't be overcome with His help. If God brings us a trial, He will bring us out of the trial. I do know when we bow to God's authority; He will bring forth a harvest from our seed. Our sweat and tears alone begin the watering process! When we work for God, we are one day closer to getting our miracle.

Realize today the efforts you have put forth for your child were seeds that needed to be planted. Your sweat and tears are watering those seeds. Someday, you and I will sing songs of joy when God recovers our children.

Day #30

"When you pass through the waters, I will be with you, and when you pass through the rivers they will not sweep over you. When you walk through the fire, you will not be burned; the flames will not set you ablaze. For I am the Lord, your God, the Holy One of Israel, your Savior."

Isaiah 43:2-3

To pass through means we are to move from one place to another place with purposeful intent. Meaning we are to leave the pit of autism, with our child. Our waters are the trials of autism. Today's verse promises us that Jesus is with us on this journey and that which we pass through will not destroy us.

Today's verse also says when we walk through the fire, we will not be burned. What are some ways we get burned? One way is to do nothing to move our children forward, out of the pit of autism. Another way is to listen to or practice dabbling in false ways to help our children. I have unfortunately seen some parents stay in the fire. That is when you get burned. We are to walk through the fire and into a better place than where we started.

The early years were definitely the roughest for us, as it is for most families. Before I had a handle on our sons' diet and figured out how to get supplements into him, I was floundering. I didn't know quite what foods to feed him. All I knew was the food in my pantry was acting like a poison to his body. Wrong foods in our son, led to tantrums that lasted for hours, uncontrollable crying, odd behaviors, biting, flapping of the arms and he acted spacey! It was so hard because he craved all the wrong foods that his body could use.

In those times I felt like I was up to my neck in a river, so close to being swept away. All I could do was pray. I prayed for safety, wisdom, love and for Jesus just to be near to us.

God didn't always quickly recede the deep waters I felt like I was in. But He did remind me how to stay afloat! He calmed my anxiety and I felt like He was right in the river holding onto me. I read a story once where God let the river swell, just so someone could see Him walk on water!

God did lead us to a great Defeat Autism Now doctor and he has helped us immeasurably. To get our son chemically balanced was no small feat. God led me to books to read on diet interventions and to moms who were going through the same thing I was going through.

Scriptures are ours to claim. When we read, memorize and meditate upon them, they will restore our hope. Today, know that you and I are not in this situation alone. God is here to help us walk through to a better place. We just have to keep on seeking God. Think about the place God will put you when you come out of this fire.

Day #31

"When the disciples saw Him walking on the lake, they were terrified. 'It's a ghost,' they said, and cried out in fear. But Jesus immediately said to them: 'Take courage! It is I. Don't be afraid.' 'Lord, if it's you,' Peter replied, 'tell me to come to You on the water.' 'Come,' he said. Then Peter got down out of the boat and walked on the water to Jesus. But when he saw the wind, he was afraid and beginning to sink, cried out, 'Lord, save me!' Immediately Jesus reached out His hand and caught him. 'You of little faith,' He said, 'why did you doubt?'"

Matthew 14:26–31

To take courage means to be able to face danger with confidence, resolution and bravery. If we are of 'little faith' then it means we have lost our trust and belief that God will sustain us.

When Peter took his eyes off of Jesus he began to sink. When his eyes were on Jesus, he weathered the storm. Raising our children can be a stormy season. When I pray to God to ask Him to stop this storm or take us out of this storm, He hasn't done it like I was hoping He would! But just like with Peter, Jesus comes to us while we are in the storm. He will help us get through it, if we keep our eyes on Him.

There are days when the wind is whipping at me, I am drenched in tears and all I hear is scary thunder. But when I pray and read God's Word, I weather the storm. On the days I take my focus off of God and focus on how hard autism is making our life, I truly begin to sink into a sea of fear. I think I am more like Peter than I care to admit!

I can clearly remember days when our son was so overtaken by yeast infections that he had zero self-control. He once slammed a door so hard that he broke the wooden door frame. He literally flipped the couch over. He ran threw the house breaking anything and everything he touched. God didn't calm those storms. But He did jump in and give me wisdom on how to handle Zack. And calmed the storm that was in me! I knew that God was in this storm with me; we were not and are not weathering this disorder alone. I would surely drown if I went this alone.

We can learn to feel God's presence and His peace even in our most difficult days. The Bible tells us God never abandons us. Choose to remember this today. Let God be your refuge if you are in a storm. Keep your eyes on Jesus and keep your faith! Tell God today you will do your best to have more faith in Him.

Day #32

"See that you do not look down on one of these little ones. For I tell you that their angels in heaven always see the face of my Father in Heaven. What do you think? If a man owns a hundred sheep, and one of them wanders away, will he not leave the ninety-nine on the hills and go to look for the one that wandered off? And if he finds it, I tell you the truth, he is happier about that one sheep than about the ninety-nine that did not wander off. In the same way your Father in heaven is not willing that ANY of these little ones should be lost."

Matthew 18:10-14

Today I chose to focus on a parable in the Bible called, 'The parable of the Lost Sheep.' Remember that a parable is an earthly story with a heavenly meaning. Today's parable pertains very well to parents. My husband and I have three children. Just our middle child has autism. Our other two children are normal developing.

When you have one child that requires more money, time and effort than the others, fairness goes out the window. Today's parable helps me understand that you give each child what they need. We are very much off searching for our one lost sheep.

We need to go out of our way to help siblings not feel cheated. We must help them understand we would do the same if they were the child afflicted with autism. There is nothing like life experiences to help one grow up and mature! I do everything in my power to make sure our other two children do not grow up bitter or resentful. In fact, I pray they are learning compassion, understanding and hope that will serve them well in their futures. I tell them often I would do no less for them than I do for their brother.

Our spiritual lesson is for us to give each of our children

79

what they require to be all God has designed for them to be. To teach our entire family it is all for one and one for all. Today, remember to keep looking for your stray sheep. It is okay to leave the ninety-nine behind for awhile and search for your child that is lost. If you have other children that are not on the autism spectrum, tell them you would do no less to help them overcome. Ask God to open their eyes and see your example. What a great life lesson for them!

Day #33

"Now I am about to go the way of all the earth. You know with all your heart and soul that not one of all the good promises the Lord your God gave you has failed. Every promise has been fulfilled: not one has failed."

Joshua 23:14

As Joshua was about to die, he gathered the elders, leaders, judges and officials to remind them of how God always fulfills His promises. Are there days when you feel God is not listening to your prayers? Days when you wonder if He is looking down at what is happening with your child? Today's verse reminds us that God fulfills His promises. Choose to base things on what you know and not on what you feel. Because the truth is God does hear every prayer you send up and He sees everything! Sometimes God is just silent with His answers.

God has His reasons for being silent. God is not silent because He is being mean. He is not silent because He is busy helping someone else. His silence does not mean denial to our prayers. I think God wants each of us to get to a point when we're so desperate for answers that when answers come, we know that they came from God and God alone. God doesn't like to share the glory. Silence stretches our faith and teaches us to trust God beyond what we already know about Him. God's ways cannot be explained.

God hears our prayers to Him. And He also knows our heart. God knows our deepest needs and our deepest desires. But God wants us to come to Him other than to just give Him a list of our wants and needs. When we pray, it is our way of communicating with God. He wants us to talk with Him everyday. He wants us to talk to Him about everything. He does not want us to pray to Him only when we are in need.

God has four ways of answering our prayers. He can say, "No. I love you to much." He may answer, "No, not yet." He may answer, "Yes, I thought you would never ask!" God may answer, "Yes, and here's more."

We need to continue to challenge autism. Seek out ways to help our children to learn how to talk, how to communicate, how to socialize and do all the things they do not know instinctively. I believe parents of autistic children are raised up and are chosen to fight for our children. The dreams and hopes we have for our children are put in our hearts by God. We need to pull ourselves up to meet this challenge.

God isn't happy to see us suffering. But He does love to see us grow in our faith. There are times God allows us to struggle in order to build our character. God often uses bad things that happen in our lives to bring glory to Himself. Developing our faith in God comes when we chose to believe Him at His word. When we don't feel hope, can't see any answers and no one's dishing out remedies that are working for our kids, that's when we need to exercise our faith!

If we choose to believe God and His promises with all of our heart and soul, God will exercise His power. God's Word is not false hope. Today, remember not one of God's promises have ever failed.

Day #34

"About the ninth hour Jesus cried out in a loud voice, Eloi, Eloi, lama sabachthani? Which means...My God, my God, why have You forsaken me?"

Matthew 27:46

Forsaken means to give up on, renounce, to desert, abandon or reject. Christ, God's own flesh and blood, a part of the trinity, actually felt forsaken by God, His father. He felt abandoned, rejected.

Have you ever thought that God sat in silence as you cried out to Him? I know I have. I prayed, "Our son needs You, God. He needs a healing touch from You. Do you understand that it's my/Your child, God? Why are You being silent in such a time of need?"

It's then we need to remember today's verse. Christ hung on the cross and cried out to God too! Christ cried, "My God, my God why have You forsaken me?" Christ's cry was as loud and heartfelt as mine. In fact, Christ's cry must have been a million times louder than mine. Christ cried out for all of us. I cry out for just one child. And as He cried out, God was silent. God knew He had to let His Son die on the cross. He knew the sins of the world and the sins of all future generations needed to pass through His Son's body. Without that, all of His children, you and me included, would be lost forever.

A sacrifice had to be paid. God can't be with sin. After the sacrifice, after Christ went through death on the cross, God exercised His power. Christ arose from the dead. This shows us God did not remain silent. When Christ died on that cross, He gave ALL that was needed to overcome autism. He gave all that was needed to overcome any disability, any hardship. By dying on the cross, Christ demonstrated the ultimate example of love. By God allowing His one and only Son to die, our relationship with God could be restored.

When God's time frame is not the same as our time frame, which it is often not, we tend to jump to the conclusion God is not answering our prayers. This is not true. God in His infinite wisdom is fully aware of our desires and needs. His plan is perfect. We need to remember He wants to be glorified. He wants the credit for our children being healed. He takes us on the path that will bring Him the most glory. Days, weeks and even years is all we know as humans. But God works on the scale of eternity. Eternity is something we don't think about on a daily basis. We think in terms of instant gratification, instant healings.

So if God is being silent with your prayers, remember… He has a reason. We don't have to know that reason right now. God did not forsake His Son, Jesus. God has not forsaken you, me or our children. Remember the silence will not last forever. God will make His move and the answer will be more than what we are praying for! Today, think about how God has not forsaken you or your child.

Day #35

"We are hard pressed on every side, but not crushed; perplexed, but not in despair; persecuted, but not abandoned; struck down, but not destroyed."

II Corinthians 4:8-9

There seems to be seasons in our lives that are very hard to go through. It's all the more reason to stay connected to God. When we hook up to God, He works on our behalf. I believe the best part of life is not behind us, it is not now, but it is yet to come!

In the early years, I knew nothing of the special diet our son would need to be on. I knew nothing of a cranial sacral therapy, occupational therapy, speech therapy, vitamin supplements, chelating, hyperbaric oxygen treatment and absolutely nothing of immune and gut disorders! I was perplexed, lost and confused.

But I talked with a DAN (Defeat Autism Now) doctor, whom I trusted. I read one book at a time. I networked with other parents and I continuously prayed. God did not abandon me and the devil did not destroy me. We implemented what we could, when we could and our son's behaviors improved over time.

What we needed to know in raising a child with autism is not learned in any parenting book. We must forge our way through the fear we feel. We need to be determined to find answers. Hope returns when we know God is in control. God has asked us to go forward into what is unknown to us. To figure out what we do not yet know. We are a generation of parents seeing an autism epidemic.

Today's verse instructs us not to be crushed or in despair. God has not abandoned us in our time of need. The only way autism can destroy a life or a family is if we allow it to happen.

If our source of strength and hope is in God, then our families will stay in tact.

We may be angry, but we're not crushed. We may be perplexed but we are not in despair. We may have hard days, but we are not going to abandon our children. Autism may have struck our homes, but we will not be destroyed, for God is still in control.

When you pray today, acknowledge to Jesus that you know God is in control. Thank Him for any new developments in your child. Thank Him for giving you wisdom, strength and your child. Tell Jesus you know it is because of Him you are not destroyed.

Day #36

"For it is commendable if a man bears up under the pain of unjust suffering because he is conscious of God."

1 Peter 2:19

Bear up means to carry one's person. Meaning it is commendable to carry our children through the pain and unjust suffering of autism. To be conscious of God means we are aware of God's existence.

I quickly learned my pain of having a child with autism would eat me alive if I didn't turn that pain into power. I need knowledge. Knowledge is power. I know in my heart our son was designed for so much more than what most people see in him. If I don't take the time, energy and spend the money to realize our son's potential, then that will be a debilitating pain.

Did you know God has twelve different names? Each name describes who He is. One name wouldn't cover all who God is. Two of the names are very important to you and me. Jehovah-Rophe (found in Exodus 15:26) means "My Healer." Jehovah-Nissi (found in Exodus 17:15) means "My Victory." If we want to know our God, the God we're asking to heal our kids, we need to know all we can about Him. He is the healer and He has a separate name to speak to that part of Him. God always finishes and wins at whatever He sets out to do. Our victory over autism will be because we turned to and trusted Jehovah-Nissi. Our kids will be healed because of Jehovah-Rophe.

God is a very good record keeper. He knows the time that you spend praying, reading, teaching and fighting for your child. All that we do for our children does not go unnoticed by God. God knows the ways that it costs us to press on. All our efforts and love that we put toward our children is exactly what God wants from us. We are to bear up and carry our children. God will supply all that we need to carry on.

It takes faith to unpeel the layers that are upon our children. God promises healings, and as sure as I breathe today, I know that each and everyone of our children will someday be healed of autism. When you pray today, address God by one of His names that we talked about today. He will be pleased that you are getting to know Him more intimately.

Day #37

"All things work together for the good of those that love the Lord."

Romans 8:28

Something good has to become of all that we are forced to go through. This is a trial that is long, all encompassing and just down right hard. Never have we worked so hard for such little results.

God is definitely shaping us. Shaping us to be more like Him. More patient. More forgiving. More understanding. More tolerant. I have found when I fall to my knees at night, because I haven't a clue as to how to keep going on, I am in the perfect position to pray! "Lord, tell me what to do next. Teach me how to reach my child. Show me how to teach my child. Don't let me waste the huge opportunity that You have given me to do the right thing." Ever prayed a prayer like that?

In pondering the question, "Why us, why our child, God?" the answer becomes a little bit clearer. God needs parents who will turn to Him, and only Him, for answers to autism. If we don't succeed at getting our son over autism, and we put all our faith in God to guide us, God isn't glorified. God wants to be glorified through our testimony.

I remember my parents telling my husband and me, "the bigger the need, the bigger the testimony." Whoa, the testimony we were going to have, I thought! But they were right. God loves us, loves our son and God wants to give us the desires of our heart. With so many families going through the trial of autism, the devil can have a heyday tearing families apart. Financial destruction threatens us because we take on loans, cash in on our retirements and mortgage our homes.

89

We all have valid reasons why God shouldn't have chosen us! Very few have the natural patience it takes to raise our children. Even fewer have the money that is needed to give the child every opportunity to overcome. And I don't know anyone who was a teacher of special needs, a doctor, a nutritionist and a cutting edge scientist all trained and ready to take on the challenge of autism! God is using a group of people to discover all we need to know.

We have to get on our knees and talk with God daily. We need to ask for direction, patience and to keep our hope high. Today's verse drives home the fact that God promises ALL things, including autism, will work together for the good of those of us who love God. God has probably said, "Why not you? Why not your child?" He knows we will do right by our children and He will do right by His.

Memorize today's Bible verse. Write it down and stick it where you'll see it several times today. Tell God you trust Him to work all things together for His good.

Day #38

"Be self-controlled and alert, Your enemy the devil prowls around like a roaring lion looking for someone to devour."

1 Peter 5:8

Today's verse gives us a great word picture. Picture this starving lion in the jungles of Africa. He is lurching in the shade trees and shadows for the perfect moment to pounce on some weak, unsuspecting animal. If the animal is not watching and has no plan of escape and no back up, it doesn't stand a chance to survive.

Satan is always looking for prey to devour. Lurching in the shadows for the perfect moment to move in for the kill. Today's verse tells us to be alert so we don't get devoured. To be devoured means to be eaten alive. To be alert means that we are attentive and watchful. When things are not going right, please don't be afraid to name the trouble. It is Satan who brings the trouble.

Grieving over our sons' diagnosis was not a sin. But allowing Satan to paralyze my life for one and a half years was. Satan did not inhabit our lives. He did, however, bring on doubts, thoughts of inability, and insecurity. I was so busy grieving over the prospect of our future I did not watch for the roaring lion that was seeking to devour me.

I was very short sighted in thinking our son had this bleak future. When his doctor told us, "Your future road is long and dark and not one of much hope," I was devastated. Satan used lies to break my spirit. Lies are all that Satan has. So, he has to be very good at making us believe them!

We have to have faith in God's ability to help our children overcome autism. God has the ability to accomplish what doctors, teachers, scientists and parents cannot. When we open our hearts, God opens our eyes. We must see Satan's lies for what they are. We know God's truths and His promises if we take the time to read our Bible.

If we live our lives being tired, negative or stressed there is no way we will have self-control and be alert. Self-control means we have control over our emotions, desires and actions. It is our responsibility to get the rest we need and be disciplined with all we need to do. With our eyes open, truths jump from Scripture. Hope abounds and love is winning! Autism is not too big for our God.

Today, examine your thoughts. Get rid of any lies Satan has you believing. Be very alert for the enemy.

Day #39

"For God, who said, 'Let light shine out of darkness,' made His light shine in our hearts to give us the light of the knowledge of the glory of God in the face of Christ."

II Corinthians 4:6

A verse scripted for those of us walking on a long dark road! I remember vividly the night our former family practice doctor talked to my husband and me about our son having autism and Neurofibromatosis. I remember his haunting words, "Your road is going to be a long, dark and a very rough road. I hope you can find some light along the way." Words carved forever on my hurting, broken heart.

But years later, I know God has used and continues to use my husband and I to encourage other parents on this same journey. Light is very much available. Even though the road is not lit very far ahead of each step that I take, there is light on my road. It takes faith and trust in God to daily forge on.

My human mind struggles as the world tells me there is no cure for autism. The world tells me God is not enough. Thank goodness for the Bible, for it reminds me that He is enough! God's love reaches our deepest need. His power is not limited to raising Christ from the dead.

Have you ever been in a pitch black room? If you're in that dark room and someone lights a match, where do your eyes immediately go? Directly to the light. Light cannot be hidden in total darkness. In fact, the darker it is, the brighter the light shines.

On a regular basis, we can turn on the TV, pick up a newspaper or a magazine and read someone's opinion that autism is not curable. That autism is on the rise and vaccinations do not cause autism. I was told that autistic children are doomed for a life of institutions, anti-psychotic drugs and group homes. It is reported autistic children are bankrupting parents, ruining marriages and straining family relationships. This is all dark news. It is targeted at draining our hope. These are all dark lies.

It is time for families to speak about how God is sustaining them. God is meeting their needs. God restores our hope. God is lighting our path one step at a time. God is not allowing every family to be broken apart but strengthened. God is to be turned to, not away from, or blamed when a child is diagnosed with autism. Today, look around you. Think of how you are God's light in your part of the world. You are to be a light in the part of the world that God has placed you in.

Day #40

"He will respond to the prayer of the destitute, he will not despise their plea."

Psalms 102:17-18

The word destitute refers to a person who is down. The word despise means to reject or refuse. We are not insignificant or worthless to God.

God loves us and our kids. He loves that we are seeking Him for answers to helping our kids. Why do some children recover from autism and while others are not recovering? Does God love one child more than He loves another child? No! God's healing has nothing to do with loving one child more than another.

Today's verse promises that God responds to our prayers. We must abolish the thoughts God 'might' answer in our prayers. Today's verse promises that God WILL respond to our prayers. This means He will give us an answer...hopefully someday, the answer we want to hear. So, if our child has praying parents (which they do) and parents who are seeking answers from God (which we are) then we have every reason to believe that God will be faithful to us.

I believe having a child with special needs is a test of fire. Who are we going to turn to? What kind of sacrifices are we willing to make? How much is too high of a price for us to pay in helping our children? I hope we are strong enough to remind our hearts that God is allowing what has happened to our children for a huge eternal purpose.

There is no way to have a rainbow without rain. We cannot feel joy if we have never experienced sorrow. I truly believe the deeper the hurt the sweeter the joy will be when it comes. We can let the wind knock us down or we can lean into it and let it blow our doubts and fears away. David never would have been King if he hadn't fought Goliath. We will never have a powerful testimony if we don't experience a big trial. Autism has driven us to improve our prayers and get to know our God better.

As I look out my windows, I see my yard lined with rose trees. It does not matter if I see dormant rose trees or trees that are spilling over with roses. All year long I am reminded that God responds to His children's prayers. I pray that as you finish this forty day commitment to learning more about God's word, your faith is stronger than when you began. I pray God has given you a remarkable improvement in your child's development: An improvement that was undeniably given to your child because you were faithful to God.

Today when you pray, thank God for seeing you through this study. Tell others what God has done for you and your child.

ACCEPTING CHRIST AS YOUR LORD AND SAVIOR

The Bible teaches us God sent His Son, Jesus Christ, to save our souls. God wants to spend eternity with each and every one of us. You must understand that God cannot be with sin. Every one of us is sinful in nature. In order for God to spend eternity with us, a sacrifice needed to be paid to cover our sins. God sent Jesus to pay that sacrifice. Jesus' blood was shed on the cross to cover our sins. After three days in the grave, Jesus rose from the dead. He returned to heaven and will someday come back to take us with Him. When Christ died, it allowed each and everyone of us to have a way back to God. All you have to do is say the sinner's prayer to become a Christian.

Pray this prayer or a similar one: "Dear Lord Jesus, I am a sinner. I believe You died on the cross and rose from the dead. I believe with all of my heart Your blood sacrifice covers all of my sins. I want to live my life according to Your Word, the Bible. Please forgive me of all of my sins. Come into my heart, into my life. I love You, Jesus. Amen."

BIO SKETCH

Don't Let The Devil Take Away The Hope And Dreams You Have For Your Child!

Frustrated that there were no books on the shelves of Bible book stores that would help her find Biblical references to face the challenges of raising a child with special needs, Kathy did intense research to bring back her hope. Listening to the many popular preachers on TBN and doing personal Bible studies, she studied Scriptures to help her understand God's plan for her child's life. Doctors and teachers gave her no hope and told her to brace herself for the long, dark road she was now embarking on. Being brought up in a Christian home, graduating from Fresno Pacific Bible College and active in her local church, she knew in her heart that the God she serves is a God of mercy.

Here are Scriptures to restore your hope, strengthen your faith, and learn to be content, know that God has a plan for your child's life and to answer the questions as to why God picked you to be the parent of your child. Scriptures to promise that God is listening to our every prayer, that He is watching the work and efforts being done on behalf of our children and how to come to God when we are weary and burdened. Scriptures that will empower you to be strong, steadfast and to remember that with God, nothing is impossible.

Scriptures and stories to get you through the worst days! Learn how to take a Bible verse and give it meaning to raising and living with a child afflicted with autism. The New International Version of the Bible is used to give you answers and hope.

Kathy Medina lives with her husband, Glenn and three children Jake, Zack and Lexi in Clovis, California. Zack was diagnosed with Autism and Neurofibromatosis at age two and a half. Zack was in public education and is currently home schooled. At nine years old, Zack has made great progress by doing two and a half years of intense home schooling of Applied Behavior Analysis, then two and a half years of Son-Rise. He is currently doing Relationship Development Intervention as a home school program. Six years of chelation, dietary supplements, diet intervention, sensory integration, vision, auditory, occupational, sauna, speech, craniosacral therapies and hyperbaric oxygen treatments have put Zack on the road to recovery from autism.

Tate Publishing & *Enterprises*

Tate Publishing is commited to excellence in the publishing industry. Our staff of highly trained professionals, including editors, graphic designers, and marketing personnel, work together to produce the very finest books available. The company reflects the philosophy established by the founders, based on Psalms 68:11,

"the Lord gave the word and great was the company of those who published it."

If you would like further information, please call
1.888.361.9473
or visit our website
www.tatepublishing.com

Tate Publishing & *Enterprises*, llc
127 E. Trade Center Terrace
Mustang, Oklahoma 73064 USA